D1790667

Jimi Yamaichi
1588 Alisal Ave.
San Jose, CA 95125

庭 GARDEN VIEWS I
MODERN JAPANESE GARDENS

TATSUI TEIEN KENKYUJO

Contents／目　次

Color Plates／カラー図版 —————————————————————3

Explanalion by Takenosuke Tatsui／日本の庭園技術(龍居竹之介) ———7

Plan／庭の図面 ———————————————————————118

List／作庭家リスト —————————————————————124

Map／日本地図 ———————————————————————126

Afterword／あとがき —————————————————————127

Photographs／Osamu Nobuhara（信原 修）
English／Shigemaru Shimoyama（下山重丸）
Book design／Eikō Iwakuro（岩黒永興）

1   Maizuru Estate : Kyoto (Work of Iwao Kawahara) ～ *The stone path Nobedan connects the distance from the gate to the entrance porch.*
  舞鶴邸：京都(河原巖作品)～門から玄関までの園路は延段(石畳)で構成している

2 Sekiguchi Estate : Tokyo (Work of Zenjirō Tagomori) ~ *The both sides of the gate are given the air of soft greenery by the mixed deciduous plantings.*
　関口邸：東京(田籠善次郎作品)〜柔らかな雑木の線を生かした門の内外

3　Kobayashi Estate：Iwate (Work of Hiroshi Moniwa)〜 *The front garden is treated by the plain wooden fence and stone wall.*
小林邸：岩手（茂庭弘作品）〜素朴な木の塀と石垣でまとめた前庭

4 Takamura B Estate : Tokyo (Work of Hideo Shida)〜*In the front garden monotony is avoided by giving variety for the stone paving.*
　　高村B邸：東京(信太秀夫作品)〜敷石の扱いで変化をつけた前庭

5   Tsuji Estate：Shimane (Work of Garden Kawashima)～*Looking toward the gate from porch a delicate curving will be noticed in the garden path.*
辻邸：島根(庭の川島作品)～玄関から門の方向を見ると、園路は微妙にカーブしている

6 Restaurant Tōyōtei : Hiroshima (Work of Norimi Ono) ~ *Garden path from gate to the porch. The stone lantern to the left has its lower portion buried in the ground.*
　料亭　登葉亭：(小野登身作品)〜門から玄関への園路。左側の石燈籠は下部を土に埋込んでいる

7   Ubukata Estate : Nagano (Work of Daiichi Ryokuchi) ~ *The path to the porch is treated boldly by large stones.   The bamboo fence behind shows partition for the main garden.*
生方邸:長野(第一緑地作品)～玄関への道は大きな石を大胆に扱っている。背後の竹垣で主庭と区切る

8 Ōhara Estate：Tokyo (Work of Miki Fujino)～*Front garden has the scene of water surface by use of white sands.*
　　大原邸：東京(藤野三樹作品)～白砂で水面を表現した景色を持つ前庭

9　Kinjō Estate：Okinawa (Work of Late Shinkichi Kinjō)〜*The stone wall opposite the front garden was provided to give a unique air of the screen wall of Okinawa.*
金城邸：沖縄（故・金城信吉作品）〜沖縄独特の障壁〈ヒンプン〉の雰囲気の石垣を正面につくった前庭

10 Kasuga Estate：Tokyo (Work of Sozan Kawamura)～*Looking out from the room toward the main garden which is the dry garden with the sand representing water.*
春日邸：東京(河村素山作品)～砂で水を表現した枯山水の主庭を室内から見る

11 Kasuga Estate：Tokyo (Work of Sozan Kawamura)〜 *The main garden seen outside the room (instead of No.10).*
　　春日邸：東京(河村素山作品)〜10の主庭を室外から見る

12 Kasuga Estate : Tokyo (Work of Sozan Kawamura)～*A part of the main garden (No.10, No.11) viewed from one side. In the far end of center the Kutsunugi-ishi ("shoe-removing stone") is seen.*
春日邸：東京（河村素山作品）～10、11の主庭の部分を庭の側から見る。中央奥の石は沓脱石

13 Itō Estate：Nagano (Work of Enken)～*The main garden paved with cut stones for which various finishing was made for the surface.*
伊藤邸：長野(園建作品)～表面の仕上げを変えた切石でペーブした庭

14 Moriyama Estate : Shizuoka (Work of Zenjirō Tagomori) ~ *In the main garden cut stones were buried in slanting so as to give the feeling of movement.*
    森山邸：静岡（田籠善次郎作品）～切石を傾けて埋込み、動きを感じさせる主庭

15 Moriyama Estate : Shizuoka (Work of Zenjirō Tagomori)～*Right hand side portion of No.14. The water bowl was worked on in straight lines.*
森山邸：静岡(田籠善次郎作品)〜14の右手の部分。手水鉢も直線的に加工したものだ

16　Chōkai Estate：Chiba (Work of Kazuo Mitsuhashi)〜*In making this pond garden the Middle Age garden was in mind, where stones were placed boldly.*
　　鳥海邸：千葉（三橋一夫作品）〜石組の力強かった中世の庭を意識した池の庭

17 Chōkai Estate : Chiba (Work of Kazuo Mitsuhashi) ~ *The stone arrangement garden (No.16) viewed from the room.*
鳥海邸：千葉（三橋一夫作品）〜16の石組の庭を室内から眺める

18 Kuroda Estate : Nagano (Work of Enken) ~ *The cut-stone pavement and the pruned garde plants make an interesting contrast.*
黒田邸：長野(園建作品)〜切石のペーブと丸く刈込んだ庭木のコントラストが面白い

19 D Building Roof Garden：Tokyo (Work of Chiaki Kobayashi)～*Roof garden of the seventh floor. Combines view of the natural shape trees and the large round shape of the clipped trees.*
大東京火災海上保険：東京(小林千秋作品)～7階屋上の庭。自然の形の木と丸く大きく刈込んだ木の組合わせで構成している

20 Tea room Rakushō : Kyoto (Work of Shigeru Yamaguchi)～*The green-covered form of the main garden as seen from inside the room.*
喫茶　洛匠：京都（山口茂作品）～緑に包まれた形の主庭を室内から眺める

21 Tea room Rakushō : Kyoto (Work of Shigeru Yamaguchi)～*The branching point of garden path shown in center of No. 20. An old building foundation stone is being utilized.*
喫茶　洛匠：京都(山口茂作品)～20の中央に写る園路の分岐点。古い建築の礎石を利用している

22 Isono Estate : Tokyo (Work of Tokuji Amamiya) ~ *For winter protections, straw is used for herbaceous plants, and the fallen pine needles for mosses and lichens.*

磯野邸：東京(雨宮徳治作品)～ワラで草を、松葉を敷いて苔を、それぞれ寒気なら守る。室内から眺めた主庭の冬姿

23 Yamauchi Estate：Tokyo (Work of Kenichirō Sugiura)～*For this pond garden the main features are the pine tree on the right side of center and the bamboo to the left.*
山内邸：東京(杉浦健一郎作品)～中央の松、左側の竹垣がポイントになっている池中心の庭

24 Nakamura Estate：Nagano (Work of Motomi Oguchi)～*The two pine trees form the central view. The pond surface is symbolized by the white sand.*
中村邸：長野(小口基実作品)～2本の松が景色の中心となる。池は白砂で水面を表現している

25　Fujimoto Estate：Ōita (Work of Masao Kato)～*Garden with a 5-story pagoda as its main feature.   The distant mountain is also contributing the scene.*
　　藤本邸：大分(加藤正雄作品)～5層の石塔をメインにした庭。遠くの山の景色も生かしている

26 Akiyama Estate：Shiga (Work of Ueda Zōen)～*White sands represent the water. The stream is crossed by the stone bridge and stepping-stones.*
秋山邸：滋賀(上田造園作品)～白砂で水を表現。流れる水の上を石橋や飛石で渡る

27　Akitani Estate：Ōita (Work of Masao Katō)～*Water is represnted by the white sands.　The stone lantern on the right is of Yukimi style.*
　　明谷邸：大分(加藤正雄作品)～白砂で水を表現。右手の石燈籠は雪見形と呼ぶもの

28 Yanagisawa Estate：Nagano (Work of Akaneen) 〜 *In the main garden the deciduous planting is giving the air of nature. The bamboo fence to the left helps in controling the view.*
柳沢邸：長野(あかね苑作品)〜雑木で自然のムードを出した主庭。左側の竹の垣根が景を締める

29 T Estate : Tokyo (Work of Kotarō Terada) ~ *Looking out from the room toward the main garden which is made up of the cutstone paving and planting work.*
T邸:東京(寺田小太郎作品)〜敷石と植込みでまとめた主庭を室内から見る

30 Sugita Estate：Tokyo (Work of Mitsukoshi Dpt.)～*The terrace garden. The objet d'art "Morning sun" made by Kenji Misawa serves the key point of the garden.*
杉田邸：東京（三越作品）～テラスの庭。オブジェの『朝日』（三沢憲司作）がこの庭のポイント

31 Sasaki Estate : Miyagi (Work of Masahisa Koyama)~ *In this garden the distant and near views are combined by the bamboo fence. This is an example of Shakkei, the borrowed scene.*
佐々木邸:宮城(小山雅久作品)〜竹の垣根で遠景と近景を結びつけた庭

32　Katō Estate：Ōita (Work of Teitoku Komatsu)～*This is the "dry landscape".　The scene of water coming down from a roaring cascade runs in gorge.*
加藤邸：大分(小松貞徳作品)〜豪快な瀧から水が落ちて流れるようすを、水を使わずに表現した庭

33　Ōkubo Estate：Nagano (Work of Niwabayashi Arai Zōen) ～ *The view is made by placing the natural stone in front of the earthen wall and the 3-story stone pagoda.*
　　大久保邸：長野(庭林　荒井造園作品)～土塀の前に自然石と３層石塔で眺めをつくる

34 Nakamura Estate : Nagano (Work of Chōyūen)~ *The main garden has ground surface finished with beautifully colored sands.*
中村邸：長野（長遊園作品）〜美しい色の砂で地表を化粧した主庭

35 Fukumaru Estate：Kyoto (Work of Yoshinobu Kubo)～*The roof garden. Here some natural pieces are used for the stepping-stone path among the straight-line design.*
福丸邸：京都（久保養信作品）～屋上の庭。直線的な構成の中に、自然石の飛石も用いている

36 Ichikawa Estate : Saitama (Work of Sozan Kawamura)～*The attractive Nobedan path built in parallel with the bamboo fence of Amidagaki style.*
市川邸：埼玉（河村素山作品）～竹の垣根〈阿弥陀垣〉の前に平行してつくられた延段園路の美観

37 Kitano Estate : Nagano (Work of Oragaen)～*The ground of the main garden is finished with an interesting pattern by use of shrubs.   On the right is Kutsunugi-ishi ("shoe removing stone").*
北野邸：長野(おらが園作品)～灌木で面白い模様を地面につくった主庭。右手の石は沓脱石

38　K Estate : Tokyo (Work of Kotarō Terada)～*Piling of small stones and the bold placement of large blue stone create a new world.*
　　K邸：東京(寺田小太郎作品)～細かい石積みと、大胆な青石の配置で別天地を生む

39　F Estate：Tokyo (Work of Takeo Mitsuzono)〜 *A piece of objet d'art by Takamichi Itō is decorating the terrace made of wooden materials.*
　　F邸：東京(満園武雄作品)〜木材で構成したテラスにオブジェ(伊藤隆道作)を飾った主庭

40   Hotel Nenrinbo：Kyoto (Work of Takehiko Kawakatsu)～*In the foreground of main garden are seen Jakago or pebble-filled bamboo-baskets which serve as the bamboo material shore protection.*
ホテル　然林房：京都（川勝武彦作品）～竹製の護岸材料である蛇籠を手前に据えた主庭

41 Suzuki Estate：Tokyo (Work of Takayuki Hirai)～*A snow-covered garden scene. Stone lantern is placed in the pond.*
　　鈴木邸：東京(平井孝幸作品)～雪をかぶった庭の景。石燈籠は池の中に建ててある

42 Yamamoto Estate : Saitama (Work of Shūhei Kitazawa) ~ *Garden planted mostly with common deciduous trees.*
　　山本邸：埼玉(北澤周平作品)〜雑木を主にした庭。この生長が庭の成長につながって行く

43 Yoshida Estate：Nagano (Work of Shōwa Garden)～*The curving line made by planting of azaleas gives interest to this garden.*
吉田邸：長野(昭和ガーデン作品)～サツキの植込みがつくるカーブが、この庭の面白さである

44 Tatsuta Estate：Ishikawa (Work of Kiyoshi Nakashima)～*Here a small world is created by simply placing natural stones of various sizes to right and left.*
辰田邸：石川(中嶋清志作品)～左右の大小の自然石の配置だけで、小宇宙が生まれる

45 Ichinokawa Estate : Saitama (Work of Shunpō Matsuyama)～*The main feature of this garden is expressed by the waterfall composed of three pieces of stone at far end of the right side.*
市野川邸：埼玉(松山春峰作品)～右奥の3個の石による瀧の表現がこの庭のポイントとなっている

46 Nishikawa Estate : Tokyo (Work of Miki Fujino)～*The focus of this garden is the stone bridge set low in the center.*
西川邸：東京(藤野三樹作品)～低く据えた中央の石橋がこの庭の中心

47 Hokari Estate：Nagano (Work of Misugi Teien)〜*A bright mood is generated in the main garden by the white fence, vertical lines of bamboo and the green moss.*
保刈邸：長野(三杉庭苑作品)〜白い塀、垂直な竹、緑の苔で明るいムードの出た主庭

48   B Estate：Niigata (Work of Kōsuke Gotō)～*View of main garden from inside the room showing the stone paving and garden path.*
B邸：新潟（後藤剛助作品）〜室内から主庭の敷石や園路の姿を見る

49 Masui Estate : Hyōgo (Work of Masamitsu Kido) ~ *The main garden is made enjoyable with the Tsukubai and providing Inaho or naturalistic rice-plant-ear fence.*
増井邸:兵庫(木戸雅光作品)~蹲踞を主に右手には稲穂垣をつくって楽しめる主庭としている

50   Takeda Estate：Shimane (Work of Nagano Zōen)～*Low pine trees are planted inside of the fence in order to bring out the distant view.   The whirling of the sand surface is called Samon.*
武田邸：島根（永野造園作品）～遠景を生かすため塀の内部の松は低いものを選ぶ。砂地の渦巻は〈砂紋〉と呼ぶ

51　Ryūmon Zenji Temple：Nagano (Work of Bungobayashi Zōen)～*Garden of Karesansui or dry landscape with a hedge in background.*
龍門禅寺：長野（文吾林造園作品）～生垣をバックにした枯山水の庭

52 Chino Estate : Nagano (Work of Niwabayashi Arai Zōen)〜*Small pieces of stone buried in the sand usually represent islands.*
　　千野邸：長野(庭林　荒井造園作品)〜砂に埋もれた小石は島を表現する場合が多い

53 Morino Estate：Shizuoka (Work of Eiichi Kawayauchi)〜*Stepping-stone garden path crosses among the stream water.*
　　森野邸：静岡（川谷内映一作品）〜水の流れる間を飛石の園路が横切る

54 Takizawa Estate：Nagano (Work of Enken)～*The pond shore is made by piling the cut stones with roughly finished surface.*
瀧沢邸：長野(園建作品)～表面を粗く仕上げた切石で側面を積んだ池。白い部分は照明具

55　Sakai Estate：Ōita (Work of Hiroshi Nakamura)〜*The pond garden with the shore protection of combined natural stones.*
　　酒井邸：大分（中村宏作品）〜自然石を組合わせた護岸を持つ池庭

56　Kajiwara Estate：Ōita (Work of Keiji Kajiwara)〜*The slightly curved stone bridge helps unifying the view of the stone arrangement.*
　　梶原邸：大分（梶原敬司作品）〜やや反った石橋が石組をひき締める

57 Ikeda Estate：Nagano (Work of Misugi Teien)〜*View of a cutstone bridge across the dry garden stream.*
池田邸：長野(三杉庭苑作品)〜渓流をかたどった枯流れの中に切石の橋を渡して眺めとする

58 Yoshida Estate : Nagano (Work of Shōwa Garden)〜*Seeing the stone setting of the main garden from one side presents another view.*
吉田邸：長野(昭和ガーデン作品)〜主庭の石組を横から見ると、こちらからも1つの眺めとなっている

59　Kitano Estate：Nagano (Work of Uekō)～*By the bold placing of vertical rocks and the natural stone bridge a heavy mood is created in this garden.*
　　北野邸：長野(植孝作品)～大胆な立石や自然石の石橋の扱いで重厚なムードが出た庭

60 Watanuki Estate：Tochigi (Work of Kōji Ikeda)〜*The stepping-stone path built under deep caves gives some gentle mood.*
綿貫邸：栃木(池田幸司作品)〜深い軒の下につくられた飛石の園路はおとなしい感じだ

61 Suzuki Estate：Shizuoka (Work of Hikari Zōen)〜*Garden in front of the third floor living room. A pond is built well despite the narrow area.*
鈴木邸：静岡（ひかり造園作品）〜3階の居間前の庭。狭い場所だが巧みに池もつくっている

62 Akayama Estate : Shimane (Work of Garden Kawashima)～*Garden stream view built to give an impression of reduced natural landscape.*
　　赤山邸：島根（庭の川島作品）～自然の景色を縮小した感じにつくられた流れの景

63 Kobayashi Estate：Hiroshima (Work of Terutoshi Ikeshita)〜*Looking toward the residence from a side of garden through the plantings.*
小林邸：広島(池下照年作品)〜庭の側から植栽を通して住宅を見る

64 Yoneda Estate : Shimane (Work of Sonoyama Shōunen)〜*Viewing the stepping-stone path leading to the tea room and its surroundings.*
米田邸：島根（園山松雲園作品）〜茶室へのルートに打たれた飛石と周囲の景観を見る

65 Itsubo Estate：Nagano (Work of Seitaien Niwasei)～*This garden was built with its two sides of buildings and two sides surrounded by fences.*
伊坪邸：長野(青苔園　庭清作品)～２面を建物、２面を垣根に囲まれた中につくられた庭

66 Restaurant Yoshimura : Tokyo (Work of Nobuaki Nagai)〜*Waterfall and pond built in the court of restaurant. The plantings go well with the area.*
料亭　よし邑：東京(永井信明作品)〜料亭の中庭につくられた瀧と池。植栽もよく合っている

67 Terashita Estate : Shiga (Work of Hiroshi Terashita)〜*Court garden where an animated mood is obtained by planting Japanese sago palms seen in warm regions.*

寺下邸：滋賀（寺下弘作品）〜暖地に多いソテツを植えて豪華ムードを出した中庭

68 Imagawa Estate：Ōita (Work of Shūichi Kuriki)〜*The stone placing work centering the large natural stone was built to suit the view from inside the room.*
今川邸：大分（栗木修一作品）〜大きな自然石を中心にした石組は室内からの眺めに合うようにつくられた

69 Nakano Estate : Ishikawa (Work of Keiji Matsumoto)〜*The small space is dealt with a Tsukubai water basin and a stone lantern of Kanshūji type.*
中野邸：石川（松本啓二作品）〜狭いスペースを蹲踞と勧修寺形の石燈籠でまとめている

70 Pab La Marisco：Kyoto (Work of Yōtarō Ono)〜*The fence represents water and the boat can reach the center. Court garden of a smart design.*
パブ・ラ・マリスコ：京都（小野陽太郎作品）〜塀は波を表現、中央には舟が行く。しゃれたデザインの中庭だ

71 Nomura Estate：Tokyo (Work of Takeyuki Itakura)〜*Deciduous trees are growing from among the rocks. Such is the concept of view of this court garden.*
野村邸：東京(板倉武幸作品)〜石の間から雑木が伸びる。自然のそんな風景を写しとった中庭

72 Nishimura Estate：Hiroshima (Work of Tatsuo Ishikawa)～*Since this garden was built on artificial ground it must be made of light weight materials. Hence the difficulty of bringing the natural feeling.*
西村邸：広島（石川辰夫作品）～人工地盤の庭なので、軽い材料でつくられるため、自然の感じを出すのは難しい

73 Restaurant Taikō : Hyōgo (Work of Yoshinobu Kubo) ~ *Garden built below the corridor of the restaurant. The scene is created by bamboos and the Michishirube (Guidepost) type of stone lantern.*

料亭　太閤：兵庫（久保義信作品）〜料亭の廊下につくった庭。竹と道しるべ形石燈籠で景色を生む

74 Nakagawa Estate : Ishikawa (Work of Kiyoshi Nakashima) 〜 *The tree trunk line cleverly wraps the large natural stone.*
中川邸：石川(中嶋清志作品)〜植栽の幹の線が、大きな自然石をうまく包み込んでいる

75 Saiin Estate：Yamagata (Work of Yasuo Okuyama)～*A neat court garden with bamboos and the rough Yamadōrō stone lantern, a peculiar style of the north-east region.*
斉院邸：山形（奥山靖男作品）～竹と東北独特の山燈籠でまとめた小じんまりした中庭

76 Masaki Estate : Hiroshima (Work of Katsuya Araya)～*Roof garden built between two rooms with Tsukubai bowl as its center.*
正木邸：広島（新谷勝哉作品）～屋上の庭。2つの部屋の間につくられ、ポイントは蹲踞としている

77 Restaurant Shozankaku：Kyoto (Work of Masamitsu Kido)～*An interior garden. The central view is the stone wellcurb.*
料亭　松山閣：京都(木戸雅光作品)～室内の庭。井戸囲いの眺めが中心

78 Yamazaki Estate：Niigata (Work of Ikechū Zōen)〜*View of the stepping-stone path of free design.*
山崎邸：新潟(池忠造園作品)〜思い切りのよい扱いをしている飛石の景

79 Ogura Estate：Miyagi (Work of Masaki Kikuchi)～*The proprietor's own works of porcelain art embelish this garden.*
　　小倉邸：宮城（菊地正樹作品）～オーナー自作の陶芸品を飾った庭

80 Nishiura Estate：Tokyo (Work of Shūhei Kitazawa)～*The garden path using the straight-line tiles is the key point of this garden.*
西浦邸：東京(北澤周平作品)～瓦を用いた直線の園路がポイントの庭である

81   Nishiura Estate : Tokyo (Work of Shūhei Kitazawa)〜 *Nobedan path made of No. 80 pieces of tile.*
    西浦邸：東京(北澤周平作品)〜80の瓦でつくった延段園路を見る

82 Suzuki Estate：Niigata (Work of Endō Teien Sōsakujo)～*The garden path going through the mosses is of pleasant design.*
鈴木邸：新潟(遠藤庭園創作所作品)～苔の中を行く園路は技巧をこらしていて楽しい

83 Hashimoto Estate：Kyoto (Work of Yōtarō Ono)〜*This garden path is made up of stepping-stones and two long pieces of cut stone.*
橋本邸：京都(小野陽太郎作品)〜飛石と細長い切石２本でまとめた園路

84 　Sasaki Estate：Niigata (Work of Shōzō Ishikawa)〜*The depth of the front garden was obtained by curving the path line and increasing the number of plants.*
　　佐々木邸：新潟（石川昇造作品）〜園路をカーブさせ、植栽を多くして奥深さを出した前庭

85 Tanaka Estate : Kanagawa (Work of Kenkichi Mifune)～*The stepping-stone garden path goes through the pond. This is called Sawatobi.*
田中邸：神奈川(三船健吉作品)～池の中を渡る飛石の園路。これを〈沢飛び〉と呼ぶ

86 Mita Estate：Ishikawa (Work of Kiyoshi Nakashima)～*The garden path made of natural stone pieces. The screen fence (bamboo) on the path is Yotsume-gaki.*
三田邸：石川（中嶋清志作品）～自然石の飛石で構成した園路。途中の仕切り垣は竹の四ッ目垣

87 Moriyama Estate : Shizuoka (Work of Zenjirō Tagomori)～*The gently curving line of irregular stone paving is called Ararekoboshi ("spilling hales").*

森山邸：静岡(田籠善次郎作品)～ゆっくり左右にカーブさせた不整形の石畳。〈霰こぼし〉と呼ぶ技法だ

88 Takamura A Estate : Tokyo (Work of Hideo Shida)～*The Nobedan path made up of various sizes of natural stones can give a soft feeling by curving its line.*
髙村A邸：東京(信太秀夫作品)～大小の自然石でまとめた延段はカーブさせると柔らか味が出る

89 Ishiwata Estate : Tokyo (Work of Sozan Kawamura)～*The both sides of this Nobedan path are held by the split bamboo pieces.*
石渡邸：東京(河村素山作品)～2つ割りした竹で両側を押さえた延段のデザイン

90 Tomonaga Estate：Ōita (Work of Keiji Kajiwara)～*This garden view is made up of the betel palm trees of the South and a Korea type stone lantern.*
友永邸：大分（梶原敬司作品）～南の暖地独特のビロウジュの木と朝鮮形の石燈籠でまとめた庭

91   Restaurant Wagon : Shiga (Work of Takagi Zōen)～*Water trickling down the stone wall and the water wheel turning by that water make up the view of this garden.*
　　料亭　輪ごん：滋賀(髙木造園作品)～石垣を伝い落ちる水と、この水を受けてまわる水車がこの庭のポイント

92　A Estate：Tokyo (Work of Shūzō Ueno)～*Roppo-seki (hexagonal rock-crystal) pieces and the dwarf Ryūnohige (Ophiopogon japonicus) decorate the ground surface.*
A邸：東京(上野周三作品)～柱状の六方石と矮性リュウノヒゲで地面を彩る

93 Tsuda Estate：Chiba (Work of Mitsukoshi Dpt.)～*The objet d'art KAIKO (ocean deep) made by Kenji Misawa placed in center is also used for a wash-basin.*
津田邸：千葉(三越作品)～中央のオブジェ『海溝』(三沢憲司作)は手水鉢としても使う

94 Amano Estate : Tokyo (Work of Shūzō Ueno)～*In the beautifully spread sand a pattern is designed by use of the dwarf Ryūnohige (Ophiopogon japonicus).*
天野邸：東京(上野周三作品)～美しく敷いた砂利の中に矮性リュウノヒゲで模様をつくる。

LAWN GARDEN by Moronobu Hishikawa=Ukiyoe painter, 17C=
17世紀に浮世絵師・菱川師宣が描いた芝庭(『餘景作り庭の図』から)

EXPLANATION ———————— TAKENOSUKE TATSUI

1　Around the Gate

2　The Garden Paths

3　How to Handle the Stones in the Garden

4　Way to Handle the Water in the Garden

5　Treatment of Trees in the Garden

6　Enjoyment of the Garden

解　説 ———————— 龍居竹之介

1　門まわり

2　庭の道

3　庭の中の石の扱い

4　庭の中の水の扱い

5　庭の中の木の扱い

6　庭の楽しみ

1 Around the Gate

Most of the modern Japanese gardens do not have enough space. Consequently, the distance between the entrance gate and the front porch is short. How to make the short distance appear longer is a gardening technique of Japan.

First, try to plant as many trees as possible to create a total view. Doing so also helps increasing the general greenery. Second, give some variety for the garden path. Instead of making the short distance connected by a straight-line path, giving a slight curve to the path will give a more feeling of ease and comfort in proceeding the path (See 2, 3, 84, 1, 9).

Even when the gate and porch are on a straight line, try to give a curve for the stone pavement (4).

Third, try to avoid facing an object directly oppsite. This idea is related to the general Japanese sentiment of not to show an object in direct and complete view. The idea is also applied in making a garden path.

1 門まわり

面積に恵まれない現代日本の庭は、門から玄関までの距離も短い。それをどのようにして距離があるように見せるか、それも庭づくりのテクニックの一つである。

門の周囲にできるだけ木を植込む形も考えられる。それは緑の量を増やすことにもつながってくる。あるいは園路に変化をつける方法もある。短い距離を直進しないで、多少カーブして進むようにすれば、園路に余裕もでてくる(2、3、84、1、9)。

門と玄関が一直線上にあるときでも、園路の敷石を曲げようとする(4)。

直接、対象物に接することを避ける、あるいは完全に姿を見せたくないといった日本人の心情ものぞかれる。それは園路にもいえる。

2

4

3

84

1

9

60

45

83

85

2 The Garden Paths

The passage in gardens has the evident function of connecting the desired points to reach, but to make that walking distance an enjoyable view is art of landscaping. In the Japanese garden, we quite often see stepping-stones placed intermittently, what is called *Nobedan*, which is a short distant stone pavement path made up of natural and cut stones used either singly or in mixed manner.

Of *Tobiishi* or the stepping-stone path, the initial piece to begin is called *Kutsunugi-ishi* or "shoe removing stone", then the path proceeds (60, 45, 83). This type of path also presents its own view in the garden (73, 59). At a branching-off point of the path an old building foundation stone is placed (21). When placing the stones, the size and shape of the stone must be chosen in order to give a rhythmical view (86).

Nobedan path can be designed either in a straight line or in curvature (36, 88). Both sides are stayed by bamboo (89). Avoiding a long and monotonous line by giving a change on the way is also a Japanese technique (89, 82). *Nobedan* can be built by use of tiles also. Different kinds of stones can be used for *Nobedan* path, if necessary (80, 81).

2 庭の道

庭の道は目的地の間を結ぶ実用性とともに、その姿そのものも景色とするから、鑑賞性もある。日本式の庭の道でよく用いられるのは石を点々と打つ（打つは据えること）飛石、自然石や加工石を単独、混用した短い距離の石畳である延段がほとんどである。

飛石は建物から庭におり立つ最初の石（沓脱石と呼ぶ）に続いて打たれたり（60、45、83）、庭の中を行く道の景としたりする（73、59）。分岐点に建物の基礎石材を使うのも一つの意匠だ（21）。打つときには石の形、大きさも含めてリズムが大切である（86）。

延段は直線、曲線にこだわらずデザインできる（36、88）。両側を竹で押えてもいい（89）。長い直線を嫌って途中で変化させるのも、日本的かも知れない（89、82）。延段は瓦でもできるなど、別に石にこだわらない（80、81）。

86

21

76

73

59

8

57

56

48

29

The Garden Paths／庭の道

34

36

89

6

82

88

87

5

80

81

3 How to Handle the Stones in the Garden

The traditional way of Japanese stone arrangement is the combination of plural pieces of stones (26, 17, 68, 32, 58). Occasionally, however, stone is placed singularly to show its beautiful form (37). In either case, the idea is mostly to present the view of nature in reduced scales, or else to present some symbolic view.

For the stone arrangement work, natural stones had been used customary, but as the style of Japanese architecture has changed gradually to the western style, the changes has been brought to the treatment of the stones, namely, the appearance of the use of artificially cut stones for the stone arrangment design (13, 18, 14). There are also attempts to make a new style of Japanese garden by the combination of natural stones and cut stones (12, 11).

Pebbles and sands are considered just as important as the regular stones. Pebbles and sands are generally used to express the ocean scenery (37, 27, 43, 51, 42). The pattern made on the sand surface, called *Samon* in Japanese garden, by use of the rake, further emphasizes the expression of the sea (50,52).

3 庭の中の石の扱い

伝統的な石の扱いは、複数の石を組み合わせる方式である（26、17、68、32、58）。さらに単独でその形のよさを示すこともある(37)。いずれにしても、そのほとんどは自然景観の縮小、あるいは象徴をはかるのが狙いである。

そこで従来は自然石が多く使われてきたが、日本式建築が次第に欧米風に変わってきたために、庭の石の扱いにも変化が見られるようになった。加工石による石組デザインの登場である(13、18、14)。加工石と自然石を合わせて新しい日本式の庭をつくろうとする試みもある(12、11)。

石と同様に重視されるのは砂利、砂で、一般的に海洋の表現に利用している(37、27、43、51、42)。この砂の表面にレーキで模様をつくった砂紋は表現をさらに強調する(50、52)。

12

11

26

13

18

14

17

68

32

58

How to Handle the Stones in the Garden／庭の中の石の扱い

16

37

27

43

51

42

50

52

66

55

4 Way to Handle the Water in the Garden

The water treatment in Japanese gardens consists principally of the expression of waterfall, stream running from the upper to the lower reaches, and the pond and lake of still water. Fountains such as seen the western gardens are rare in the Japanese-style garden. Waterfalls are mostly expressed by the setting of stones (66, 55). For the garden stream, stepping-stones are frequently placed for crossing the water. This is called *Sawatobi-ishi* in Japanese garden, meaning literally "marsh hopping stone" (53).

Before entering the tea ceremony room *(Chashitsu)*, one washes hands and rinses mouth. For this a wash basin is placed, which is *Tsukubai Chozubachi* or "low wash bowl". This setting is arranged with the water-brimming stone bowl in center, and together with the traditional arrangement of the accompanying stones, presents a fine view. For that reason, regardless of the presence or absence of the tea ceremony room, or of its original function, the arrangement has become extremely popular (7, 74, 78 49). At the same time, attemps are frequently made to modernize the arrangement (35, 15, 92, 69, 93).

4　庭の中の水の扱い

日本の庭で扱う水は上から落とす瀧、上流から下流への流れ、静かに水をたたえた池泉——を表現するのが主体である。欧米に見る噴水は日本式の庭には少ない。瀧は石組によって表現することがほとんど（66、55）。流れには飛石（沢飛石という）を渡す形もよくとる（53）。

茶室にはいる前には口や手を漱ぐが、この水施設を蹲踞手水鉢と呼ぶ。この意匠は水をたたえる鉢を主としたもので、きめられた付帯設備の石とともに組むと立派な景観になる。そのため、茶室の有無、実用性の有無にかかわらず非常に多く用いられるようになっている（7、74、78、49）。反面、それをさらに現代化したいという試みも、もちろんなされている（35、15、92、69、93）。

53

62

41

54

35

7

74

15

78

92

69

93

49

25

33

5 Treatment of Trees in the Garden

It has been a Japanese sentiment from olden times to put as much greenery as possible in the garden. However, the purpoese of the use of trees is multiple. In some case carefully fostered single trees are used (25, 65), or bamboos planted for the enjoyment of their trunks (47, 75), Often miscellaneous deciduous trees are planted for the main planting in order to enjoy their seasonal changes in the view (22, 71, 28). Sometimes trees are planted to appreciate their pruned forms (19), or else to give colors in covering the ground (46, 94).

The scene created by combination of tall trees, medium and low trees, and the ground cover, finally brings a reduced-scale view of nature, but the plant materials are selected from those fitting the locality, giving the characteristic view (90, 67). Stone pagoda (25, 33). Stone lanterns, associated with trees, bring out interesting views (65, 31, 47, 75, 90).

5 庭の中の木の扱い

少しでも庭に緑を入れたいのが、日本人の昔からの気持である。しかし木の起用法はさまざまだ。一本ずつ丁寧に形をつくりあげた木（仕立物という）を使った場合もあるし (25、65)、竹の幹を楽しむようなこともある (47、75)。落葉樹主体の雑木を用いて四季の変化を特に訴えようとすることもある (22、71、28)。

刈込んだ形を楽しむ場合 (19)、地表を植物で彩る (46、94) など、木の扱いはさまざまである。

高木、中木、低木、グランドカバーの組み合わせで生む景色は、やはり自然景観の縮小に落ち着くが、用いる材料はその土地に適したものを選んでいて、それが特色となっている (90、67)。石の塔 (25、33)、石燈籠 (65、31、47、75、90) を木にあしらうとまた面白い景色が生まれる。

65

31

47

75

90

Treatment of Trees in the Garden／庭の中の木の扱い

20

10

24

64

63

23

22

71

28

61

67

19

46

44

94

6 Enjoyment of the Garden

The garden is a place where its owner finds there the rest and enjoyment. Naturally, therefore, the taste of the owner should be found there. On the contrary, however, gardens with such individuality are actually few.

For that reason, in this and the following pages, somewhat different types of garden works are introduced.

Along with the increase of highrise buildings, the space for garden has become more and more difficult to obtain. Much study has become necessary for the roof gardens (30, 72), or for the indoor garden (77).

Modernizing of old-time features has become the subject of serious studies. Examples are the use of the former river-shore protection called *Jakago* (literally "dragon basket") the bamboo basket filled with rocks (40); the water-wheel, formerly used for multiple ends (91); stone wall (38), or else the stone boat (70).

6 庭の楽しみ

庭はオーナーが憩いを得るための場所である。当然、オーナーの好みがそこにははいってくる。従ってさまざまな意匠があってよいはずだが、存外、個性的なものは少ない。

このページと次のページは、そうした意味で少し趣の違う作品を集めている。

高層建築が増加するに従って庭のスペースはさらに確保が困難になった。屋上(30、72)や屋内(77)での庭づくりにもずいぶん工夫がこらされるようになっている。

昔の川岸保護材だった蛇籠や(40)、多目的に使った水車(91)の登場する一方、石積み(38)や石船(70)の現代化にも熱心だ。

79

38

30

39

70

91

40

77

72

PLAN／庭の図面

2 Sekiguchi Estate (Work of Zenjirō Tagomori)
関口邸（田籠善次郎作品）

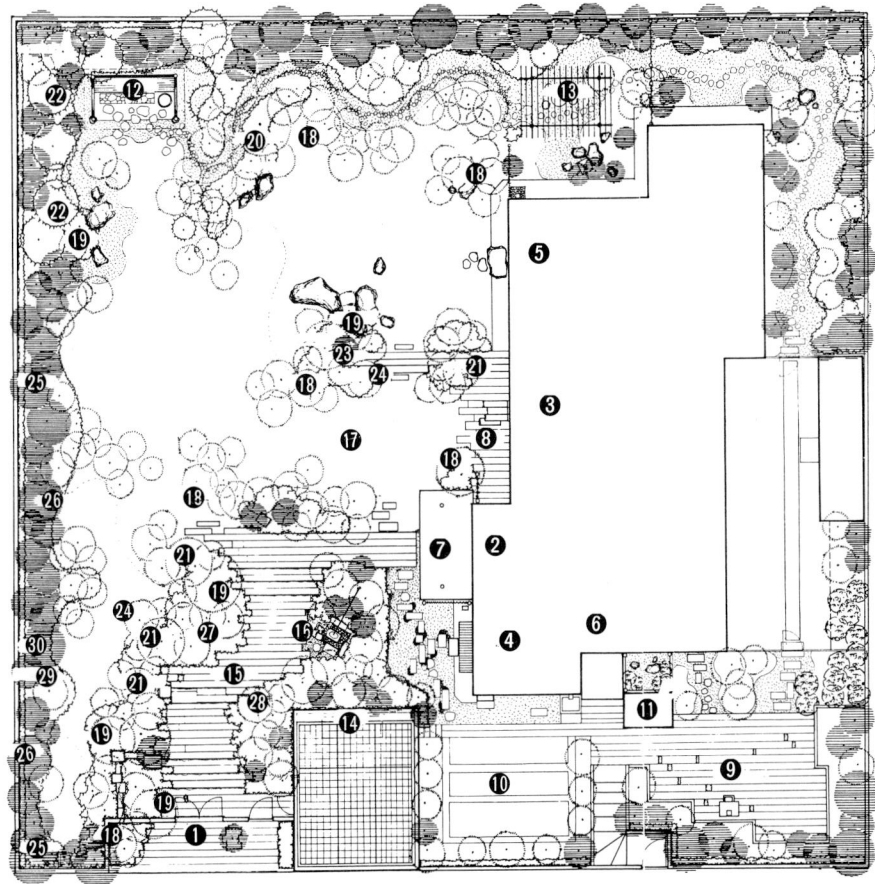

❶	GATE	門
❷	ENTRANCE	玄関
❸	RECEPTION ROOM	応接間
❹	LIVING ROOM	居間
❺	JAPANESE STYLE ROOM	和室
❻	KITCHEN	台所
❼	PORCH	ポーチ
❽	TERRACE	テラス
❾	SERVICE YARD	サービスヤード
❿	VEGETABLE GARDEN	菜園
⓫	BARN	物置
⓬	CHAIR	腰掛
⓭	WISTERIA PERGOLA	藤棚
⓮	SHELF	盆栽棚
⓯	PAVEMENT STONE	切石舗装
⓰	BIRD-BATH	バードバス
⓱	LAWN	芝
⓲	KONARA OAK	コナラ
⓳	MAPLE-TREE	モミジ
⓴	JAPANESE ZELKOVA	ケヤキ
㉑	JAPANESE STEWARTIA	ナツツバキ
㉒	JAPANESE FIR	モミ
㉓	JAPANESE ANDROMEDA	アセビ
㉔	JAPANESE DOGWOOD	ヤマボウシ
㉕	BAYBERRY	ヤマモモ
㉖	JAPANESE WHITE OAK	シラカシ
㉗	HIMESYARA STEWARTIA	ヒメシヤラ
㉘	WINGED SPINDLE TREE	ニシキギ
㉙	BIRD-LIME HOLLY	モチ
㉚	PASANIA	シイ

2 Sekiguchi Estate (Work of Zenjirō Tagomori)
関口邸（田籠善次郎作品）

2 Sekiguchi Estate (Work of Zenjirō Tagomori)
関口邸（田籠善次郎作品）

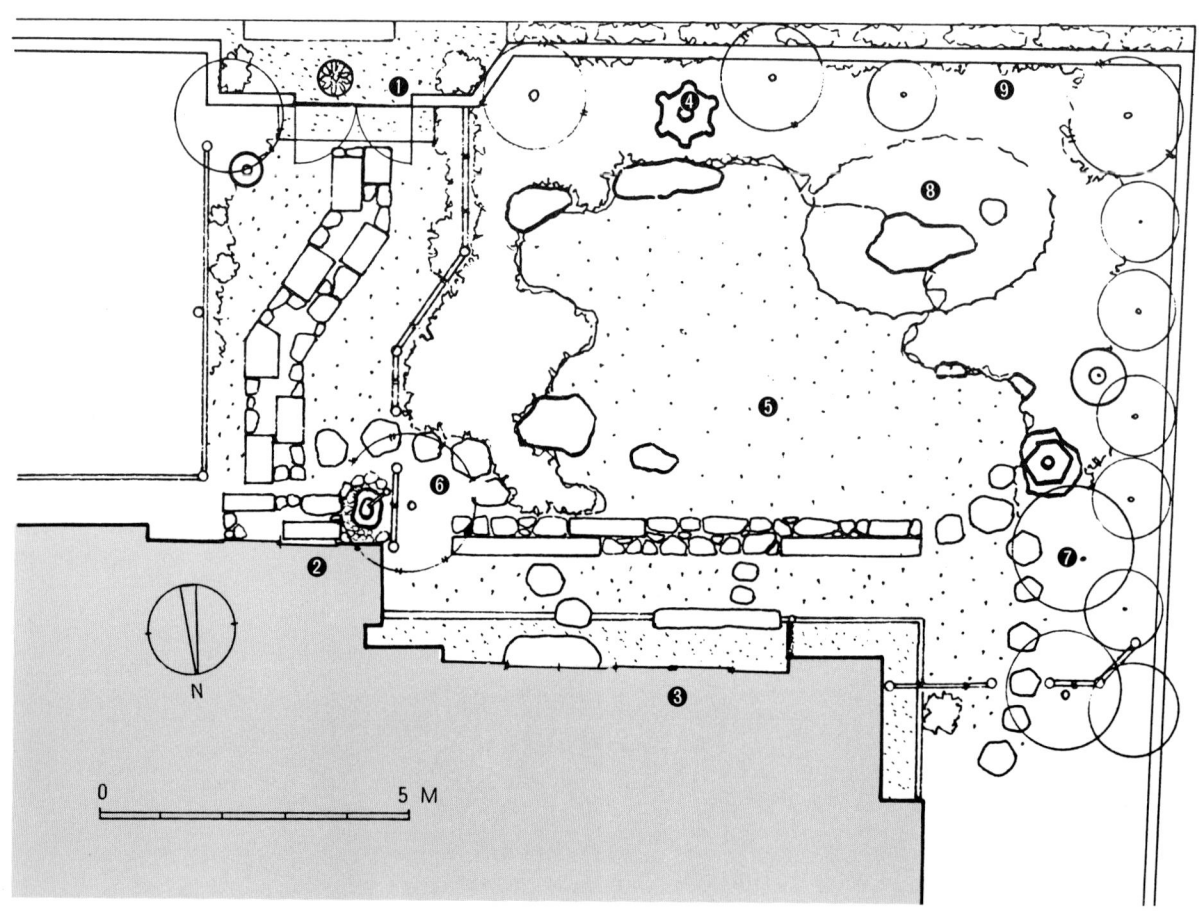

4 Takamura B Estate (Work of Hideo Shida)
高村B邸（信太秀夫作品）

❶	GATE	門	❹	STONE LANTERN	燈籠	❼	MAPLE-TREE	モミジ
❷	ENTRANCE	玄関	❺	SHIRAKAWA GRAVEL	白河砂利	❽	PINE	マツ
❸	JAPANESE STYLE ROOM	和室	❻	JAPANESE APRICOT	ウメ	❾	SHRUBBIES	株物寄植

14·15·87 Moriyama Estate (Work of Zenjirō Tagomori)
森山邸（田籠善次郎作品）

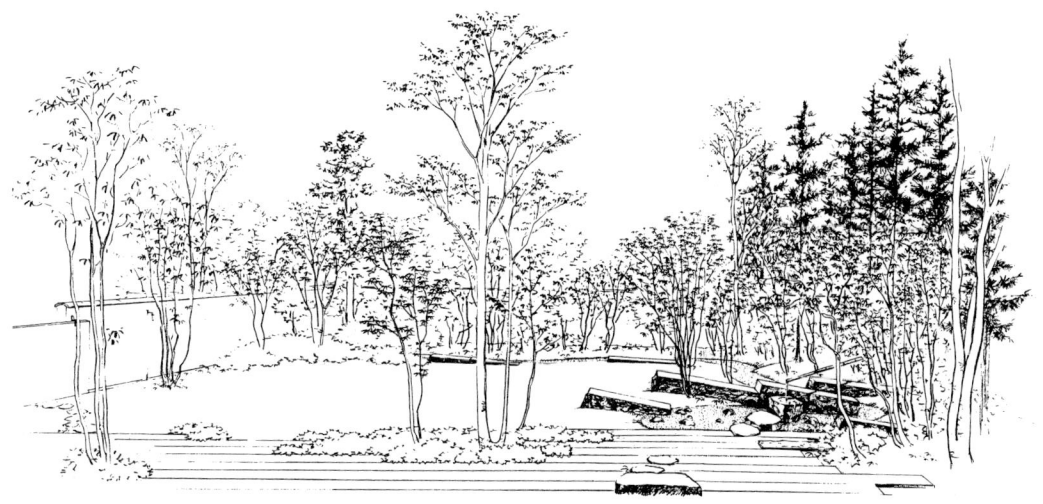

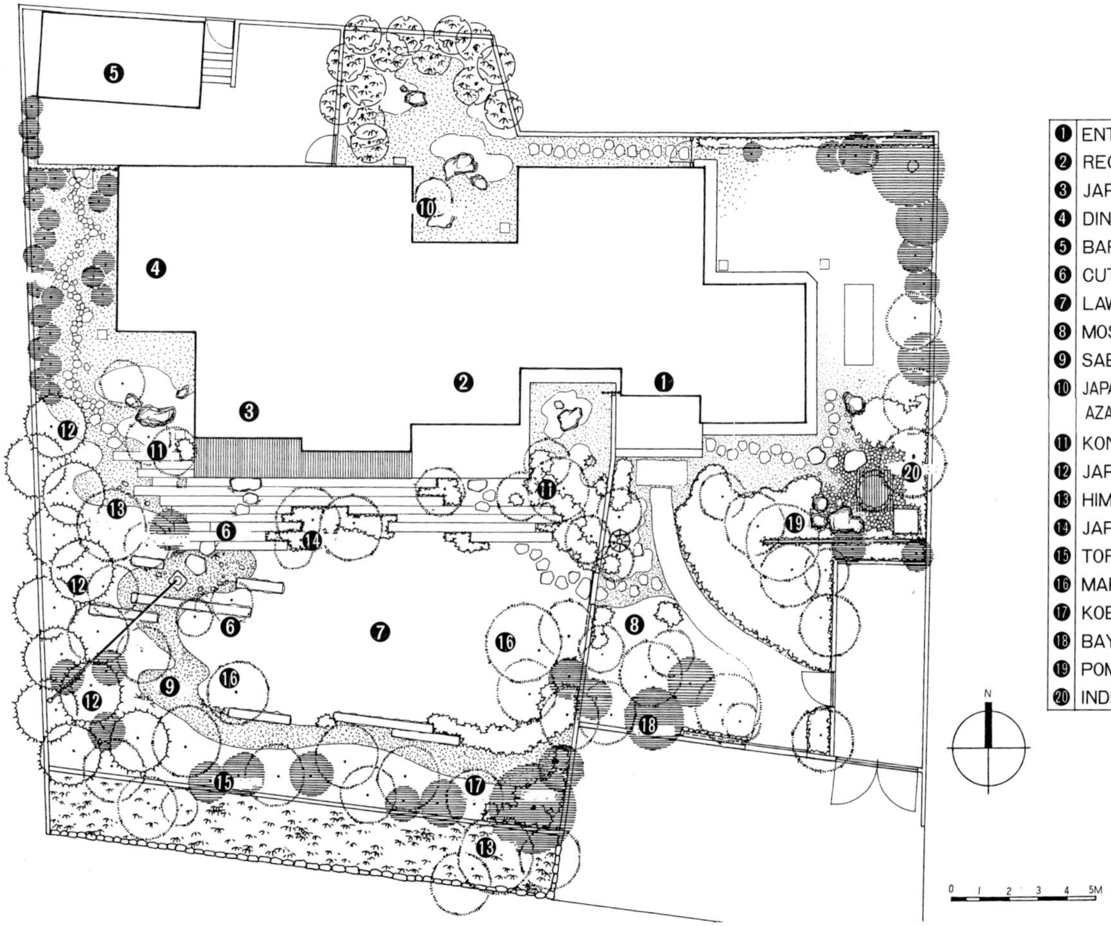

❶	ENTRANCE	玄関
❷	RECEPTION ROOM	応接間
❸	JAPANESE STYLE ROOM	和室
❹	DINING ROOM	食堂
❺	BARN	物置
❻	CUT STONE	切石
❼	LAWN	芝
❽	MOSS	苔
❾	SABIJYARI (GRAVEL)	錆砂利
❿	JAPANESE TERNATE-LEAVES AZALEA	ミツバツツジ
⓫	KONARA OAK	コナラ
⓬	JAPANESE CEDAR	スギ
⓭	HIMESYARA STEWARTIA	ヒメシャラ
⓮	JAPANESE STEWARTIA	ナツツバキ
⓯	TORCH AZALEA	ヤマツツジ
⓰	MAPLE-TREE	モミジ
⓱	KOBUS MAGNOLIA	コブシ
⓲	BAYBERRY	ヤマモモ
⓳	POMEGRANATE	ザクロ
⓴	INDIAN LILAC	サルスベリ

14·15·87 Moriyama Estate (Work of Zenjirō Tagomori)
森山邸（田籠善次郎作品）

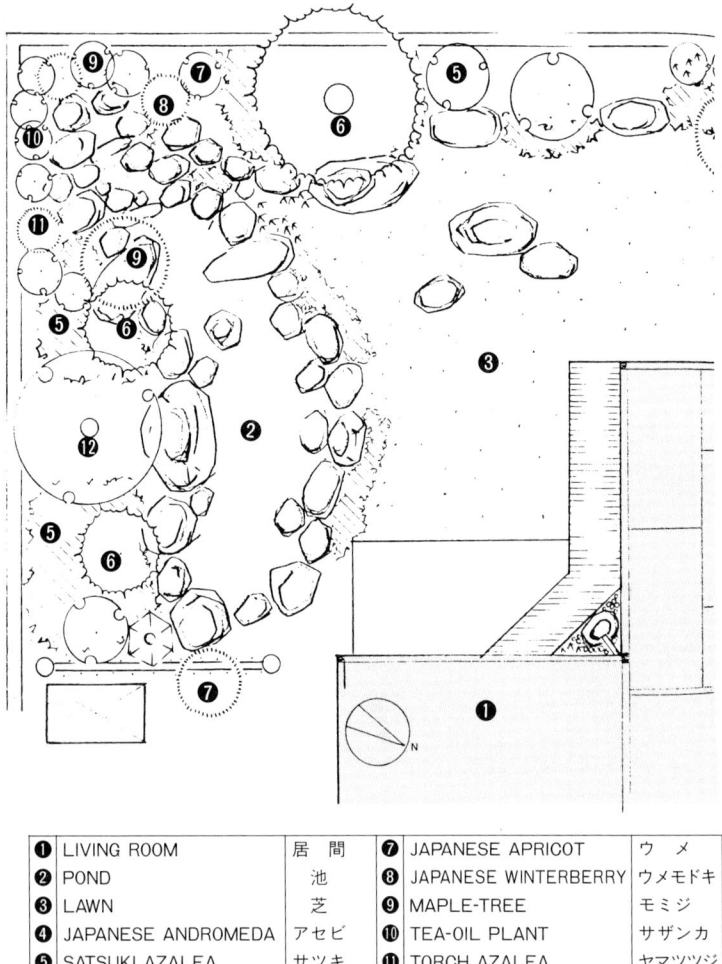

❶ LIVING ROOM	居　間	❼ JAPANESE APRICOT	ウ　メ
❷ POND	池	❽ JAPANESE WINTERBERRY	ウメモドキ
❸ LAWN	芝	❾ MAPLE-TREE	モミジ
❹ JAPANESE ANDROMEDA	アセビ	❿ TEA-OIL PLANT	サザンカ
❺ SATSUKI AZALEA	サツキ	⓫ TORCH AZALEA	ヤマツツジ
❻ PINE	マ　ツ	⓬ BAYBERRY	ヤマモモ

16・17 Chōkai Estate (Work of Kazuo Mitsuhashi)
鳥海邸（三橋一夫作品）

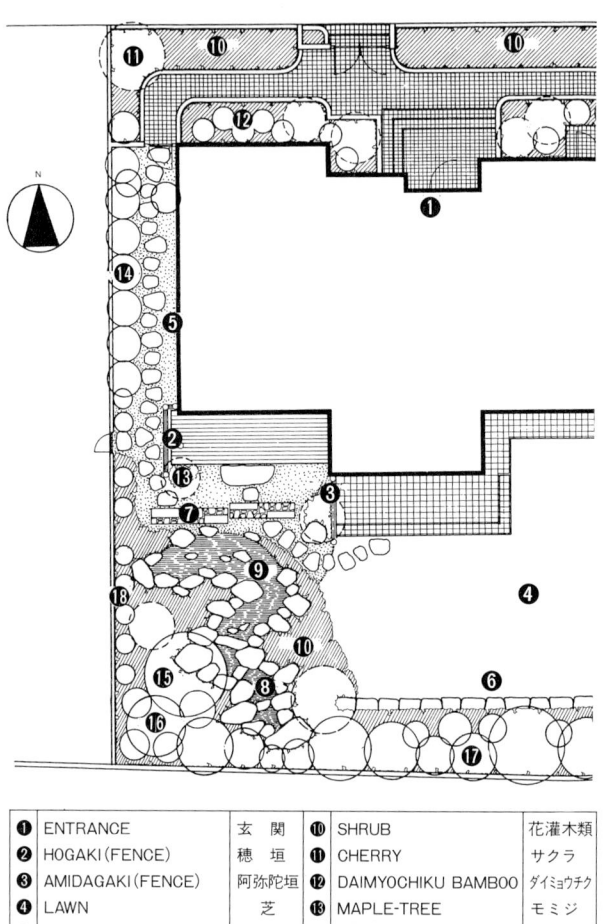

❶ ENTRANCE	玄関	❿ SHRUB	花灌木類
❷ HOGAKI (FENCE)	穂垣	⓫ CHERRY	サクラ
❸ AMIDAGAKI (FENCE)	阿弥陀垣	⓬ DAIMYOCHIKU BAMBOO	ダイミョウチク
❹ LAWN	芝	⓭ MAPLE-TREE	モミジ
❺ SAKURAGAWA PINK GRAVEL	桜川砂利	⓮ MOSOCHIKU BAMBOO	モウソウチク
❻ RUBBLE STONE	野面石	⓯ PINE	マ　ツ
❼ NOBEDAN	延段	⓰ SOUTHERN MAGNOLIA	タイサンボク
❽ WATERFALL	瀧口	⓱ COMMON CAMELLIA	ツバキ
❾ STREAM	流れ	⓲ YOSHINO JAPANESE CEDAR	ヨシノスギ

23 Yamauchi Estate (Work of Kenichirō Sugiura)
山内邸（杉浦健一郎作品）

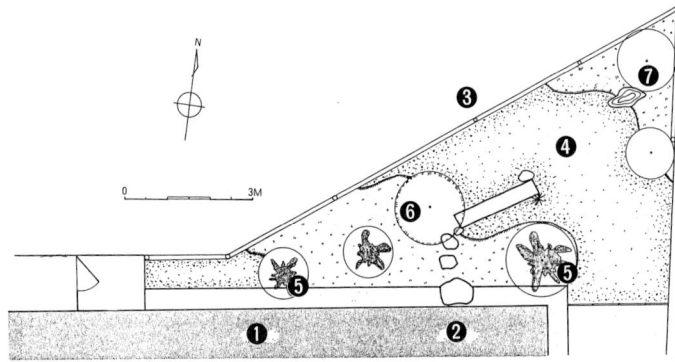

❶ LIVING ROOM	居　間	
❷ JAPANESE STYLE ROOM	和　室	
❸ MISUGAKI (FENCE)	御簾垣	
❹ SABIJYARI (GRAVEL)	錆砂利	
❺ MAPLE-TREE	モミジ	
❻ GOYŌ PINE	ゴヨウマツ	
❼ COMMON CAMELLIA	ツバキ	

46 Nishikawa Estate (Work of Miki Fujino)
西川邸（藤野三樹作品）

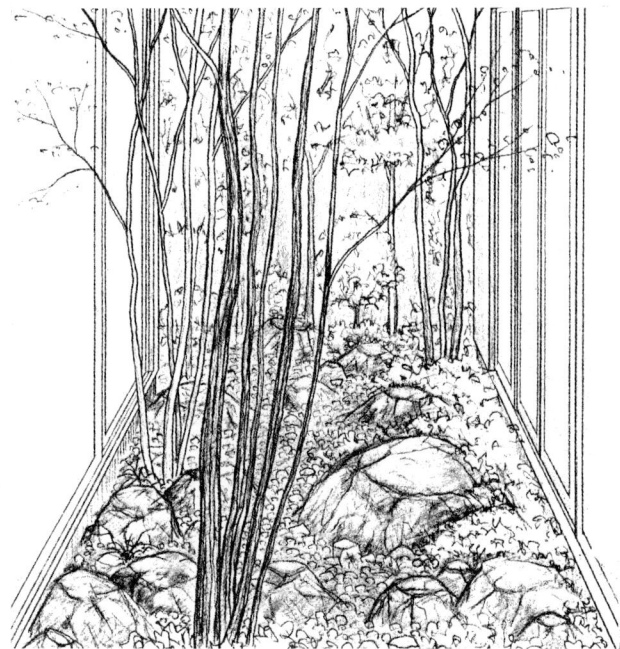

71 Nomura Estate (Work of Takeyuki Itakura)
野村邸（板倉武幸作品）

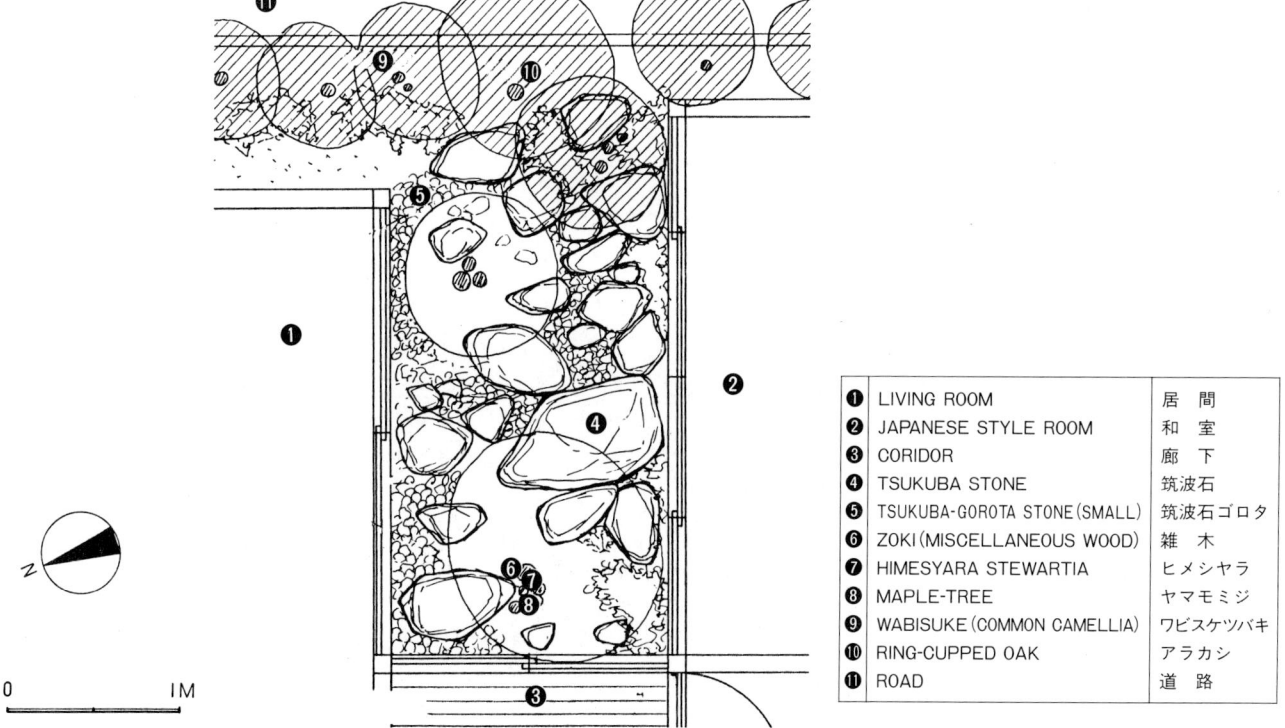

❶	LIVING ROOM	居　間
❷	JAPANESE STYLE ROOM	和　室
❸	CORIDOR	廊　下
❹	TSUKUBA STONE	筑波石
❺	TSUKUBA-GOROTA STONE (SMALL)	筑波石ゴロタ
❻	ZOKI (MISCELLANEOUS WOOD)	雑　木
❼	HIMESYARA STEWARTIA	ヒメシャラ
❽	MAPLE-TREE	ヤマモミジ
❾	WABISUKE (COMMON CAMELLIA)	ワビスケツバキ
❿	RING-CUPPED OAK	アラカシ
⓫	ROAD	道　路

71 Nomura Estate (Work of Takeyuki Itakura)
野村邸（板倉武幸作品）

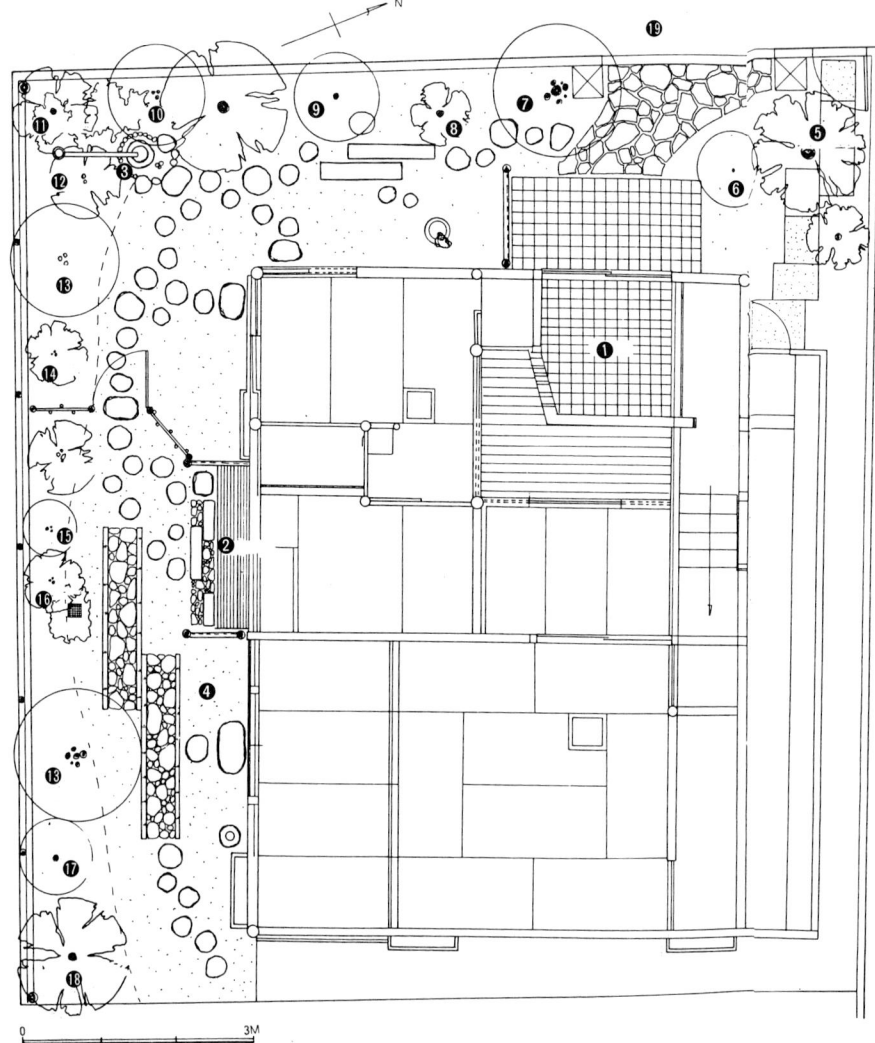

❶	ENTRANCE	玄　関
❷	CHAIR	腰掛待合
❸	TSUKUBAI	つくばい
❹	SAWARA SAND	佐原砂
❺	SOUTHERN MAGNOLIA	タイサンボク
❻	JAPANESE DOGWOOD	ヤマボウシ
❼	URIHADA MAPLE-TREE	ウリハダカエデ
❽	RING-CUPPED OAK	アラカシ
❾	JAPANESE APRICOT	ウ　メ
❿	JAPANESE SNOWBELL	エ　ゴ
⓫	PASANIA	シ　イ
⓬	JAPANESE ANDROMEDA	アセビ
⓭	JAPANESE CLETHRA	リョウブ
⓮	JAPANESE PRIVET	ネズミモチ
⓯	MAPLE-TREE	ヤマモミジ
⓰	JAPANESE AUCU	アオキ
⓱	WEEPING MAPLE	シダレモミジ
⓲	CHINESE SWEET OSMANTHUS	キンモクセイ
⓳	ROAD	道　路

89　Ishiwata Estate (Work of Sozan Kawamura)
　　石渡邸（河村素山作品）

92　A Estate (Work of Shūzō Ueno)
　　A邸（上野周三作品）

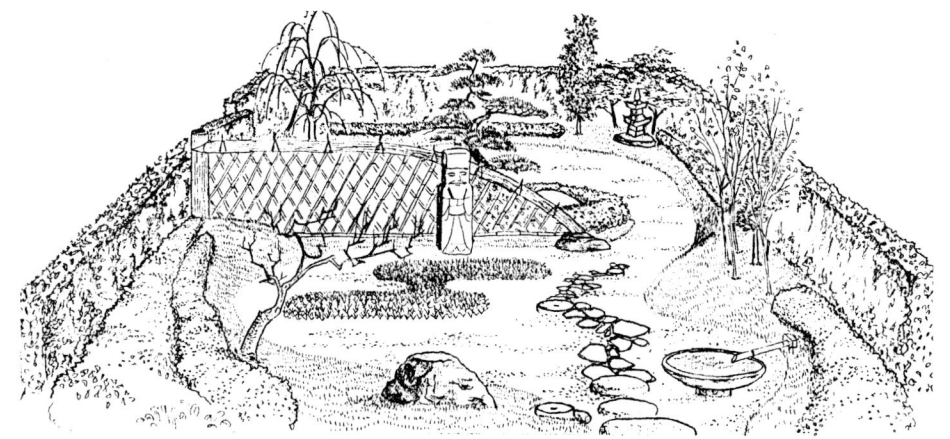

94 Amano Estate (Work of Shūzō Ueno)
天野邸（上野周三作品）

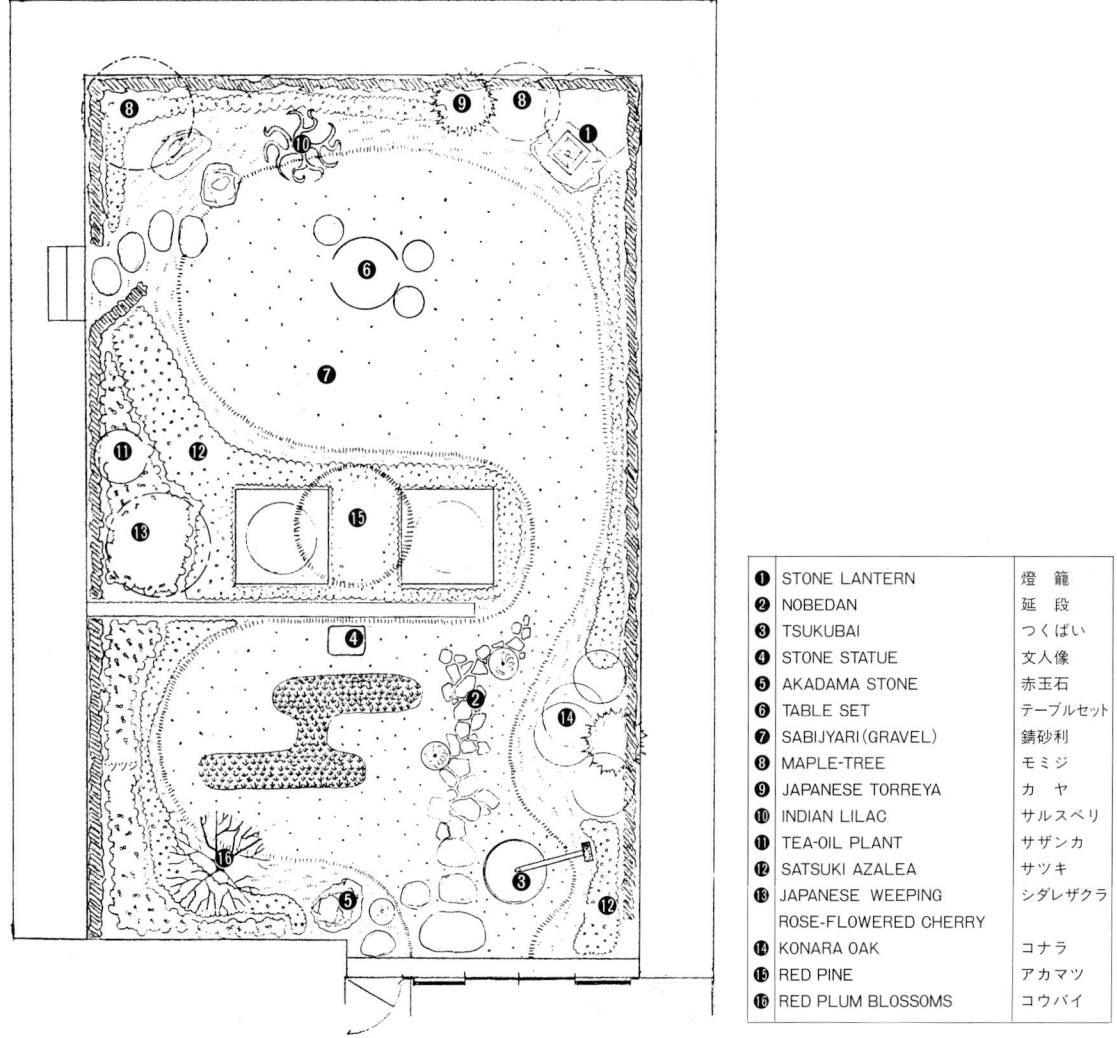

❶	STONE LANTERN	燈 籠
❷	NOBEDAN	延 段
❸	TSUKUBAI	つくばい
❹	STONE STATUE	文人像
❺	AKADAMA STONE	赤玉石
❻	TABLE SET	テーブルセット
❼	SABIJYARI (GRAVEL)	錆砂利
❽	MAPLE-TREE	モミジ
❾	JAPANESE TORREYA	カ ヤ
❿	INDIAN LILAC	サルスベリ
⓫	TEA-OIL PLANT	サザンカ
⓬	SATSUKI AZALEA	サツキ
⓭	JAPANESE WEEPING ROSE-FLOWERED CHERRY	シダレザクラ
⓮	KONARA OAK	コナラ
⓯	RED PINE	アカマツ
⓰	RED PLUM BLOSSOMS	コウバイ

94 Amano Estate (Work of Shūzō Ueno)
天野邸（上野周三作品）

LIST (GARDEN DESIGNER)

NAME (氏名)	ADDRESS (住所)	PHOTO NUMBER (掲載写真番号)
IWAO KAWAHARA 河原 巖	30 Kitachūinchō, Saganisoninmonzen, Ukyō-ku, Kyoto-shi, Kyoto 〒616 ☎075-88-5612 京都市右京区嵯峨二尊院門前北中院町30 〒616 ☎075-881-5612	1
ZENJIRŌ TAGOMORI 田籠 善次郎	1744-1 Miyama-chō, Hachiōji-shi, Tokyo 〒192-01 ☎0426-52-0174 八王子市美山町1744-1 〒192-01 ☎0426-52-0174	2, 14, 15, 87
HIROSHI MONIWA 茂庭 弘	55 Aza Ochiai, Odaki, Esashi-shi, Iwate Pref. 〒023-11 ☎01973-5-5529 江刺市愛宕字落合55 〒023-11 ☎01973-5-5529	3
HIDEO SHIDA 信太 秀夫	2-624-2 Nagabuchi, Oome-shi, Tokyo 〒198 ☎0428-22-2790 青梅市長淵2-624-2 〒198 ☎0428-22-2790	4, 88
GARDEN KAWASHIMA 庭の川島	218 Sugata-chō, Matsue-shi, Shimane Pref. 〒690 ☎0852-21-1793 松江市菅田町218 〒690 ☎0852-21-1793	5, 62
NORIMI ONO 小野 登身	8-324 Isegaoka, Fukuyama-shi, Hiroshima Pref. 〒721 ☎0849-47-0331 福山市伊勢丘8-324 〒721 ☎0849-47-0331	6
DAIICHI RYOKUCHI 第一緑地	2424 Ōaza Inoue, Suzaka-shi, Nagano Pref. 〒382 ☎0262-46-1324 須坂市大字井上2424 〒382 ☎0262-46-1324	7
MIKI FUJINO 藤野 三樹	4-9-10 Nishi-ikuta, Tama-ku, Kawasaki-shi, Kanagawa Pref. 〒214 ☎044-966-5281 川崎市多摩区西生田4-9-10 〒214 ☎044-966-5281	8, 46
SOZAN KAWAMURA 河村 素山	1-7-51 Kitano, Mitaka-shi, Tokyo 〒181 ☎0422-43-2204 三鷹市北野1-7-51 〒181 ☎0422-43-2204	10, 11, 12, 36, 89
ENKEN 園 建	3-785 Tanbajima, Nagano-shi, Nagano Pref. 〒381-22 ☎0262-84-2171 長野市丹波島3-785 〒381-22 ☎0262-84-2171	13, 18, 54
KAZUO MITSUHASHI 三橋 一夫	6-5-1 Sakushindai, Chiba-shi, Chiba Pref. 〒281 ☎0472-57-1299 千葉市作新台6-5-1 〒281 ☎0472-57-1299	16, 17
CHIAKI KOBAYASHI 小林 千秋	39 Ōaza Kyūsaemonshinden, Kawaguchi-shi, Saitama Pref. 〒333 ☎0482-95-1023 川口市大字久佐ェ門新田39 〒333 ☎0482-95-1023	19
SHIGERU YAMAGUCHI 山口 茂	7 Yamada-minami-chō, Saikyō-ku, Kyōto-shi, Kyōto 〒615 ☎075-392-6682 京都市西京区山田南町7 〒615 ☎075-392-6682	20, 21
TOKUJI AMAMIYA 雨宮 徳治	6-18-6 Honmachi, Shibuya-ku, Tokyo 〒151 ☎03-376-4583 渋谷区本町6-18-6 〒151 ☎03-376-4583	22
KENICHIRŌ SUGIURA 杉浦 健一郎	3-6-1 Mejirodai, Hachiōji-shi, Tokyo 〒193 ☎0426-63-4362 八王子市めじろ台3-6-1 〒193 ☎0426-63-4362	23
MOTOMI OGUCHI 小口 基実	2250-3 Osachi, Okaya-shi, Nagano Pref. 〒394 ☎0266-27-3069 岡谷市長地2250-3 〒394 ☎0266-27-3069	24
MASAO KATŌ 加藤 正雄	6 Honome-ku, Beppu-shi, Ōita Pref. 〒874 ☎0977-67-1044 別府市火売区6 〒874 ☎0977-67-1044	25, 27
UEDA ZŌEN 上田造園	144 Sakamoto-honmachi, Ootsu-shi, Shiga Pref. 〒520-01 ☎0775-78-0364 大津市坂本本町144 〒520-01 ☎0775-78-0364	26
AKANEEN あかね苑	93-1 Ōaza Takanashi, Suzaka-shi, Nagano Pref. 〒382 ☎02624-5-5905 須坂市大字高梨93-1 〒382 ☎02624-5-5905	28
KOTARŌ TERADA 寺田 小太郎	2-35-2 Hanegi, Setagaya-ku, Tokyo 〒156 ☎03-321-6037 世田谷区羽根木2-35-2 〒156 ☎03-321-6037	29, 38
MITSUKOSHI GREEN CENTER-BU 三越 グリーンセンター部	1-4-1 Muromachi, Nihonbashi, Chūō-ku, Tokyo 〒103 ☎03-241-3311 中央区日本橋室町1-4-1 〒103 ☎03-241-3311	30, 93
MASAHISA KOYAMA 小山 雅久	5-37 Hoshunin-maechō, Sendai-shi, Miyagi Pref. 〒982 ☎022-286-5763 仙台市保春院前丁5-37 〒982 ☎022-286-5763	31
TEITOKU KOMATSU 小松 貞徳	Nishi-nakao, Yamaga-machi, Hayami-gun, Ōita Pref. 〒879-13 ☎09777-5-6227 大分県速見郡山香町西中尾 〒879-13 ☎09777-5-6227	32
NIWABAYASHI ARAI ZŌEN 庭林 荒井造園	394 Inada, Nagano-shi, Nagano Pref. 〒380 ☎0262-41-4331 長野市稲田394 〒380 ☎0262-41-4331	33, 52
CHŌYŪEN 長遊園	903 Yamaguchi, Ueda-shi, Nagano Pref. 〒336 ☎0268-22-6746 上田市山口903 〒336 ☎0268-22-6746	34
YOSHINOBU KUBO 久保 義信	17 Ōmiya-kitayamanomae-chō, Kita-ku, Kyoto-shi, Kyoto 〒603 ☎075-492-2889 京都市北区大宮北山ノ前町17 〒603 ☎075-492-2889	35, 73
ORAGAEN おらが園	2-25-5 Uematsu, Nagano-shi, Nagano Pref. 〒380 ☎0262-32-5196 長野市上松2-25-5 〒380 ☎0262-32-5196	37
TAKEO MITSUZONO 満園 武雄	4-29-20 Azamino, Midori-ku, Yokohama-shi, Kanagawa Pref. 〒227 ☎045-902-4300 横浜市緑区あざみ野4-29-20 〒227 ☎045-902-4300	39
TAKEHIKO KAWAKATSU 川勝 武彦	41 Tschitenjō-chō, Takagamine, Kita-ku, Kyoto-shi, Kyoto 〒603 ☎075-491-2828 京都市北区鷹峯土天井町41 〒603 ☎075-491-2828	40
TAKAYUKI HIRAI 平井 孝幸	3-7-2 Shinmachi, Hōya-shi, Tokyo 〒202 ☎0422-52-1058 保谷市新町3-7-2 〒202 ☎0422-52-1058	41
SHŪHEI KITAZAWA 北澤 周平	1-15 Furuichiba, Kitamoto-shi, Saitama Pref. 〒364 ☎0485-91-0211 北本市古市場1-15 〒364 ☎0485-91-0211	42, 80, 81
SHŌWA GARDEN 昭和ガーデン	415-2 Ōaza Tomitake, Nagano-shi, Nagano Pref. 〒381 ☎0262-44-5138 長野市大字富竹415-2 〒381 ☎0262-44-5138	43, 58
KIYOSHI NAKASHIMA 中嶋 清志	130 Shimonogōmachi, Neagari-machi, Nomi-gun, Ishikawa Pref. 〒929-01 ☎0761-55-4654 石川県能美郡根上町下の江町130 〒929-01 ☎0761-55-4654	44, 74, 86

NAME (氏名)	ADDRESS (住所)	PHOTO NUMBER (掲載写真番号)
SHUNPŌ MATSUYAMA 松山 春峰	1-12-9 Matsue-chō, Kawagoe-shi, Saitama Pref.　〒350　☎0492-24-1190 川越市松江町1-12-9　〒350　☎0492-24-1190	45
MISUGI TEIEN 三杉庭苑	1057 Kotobuki-koaka, Matsumoto-shi, Nagano Pref.　〒390　☎0263-57-2569 松本市寿小赤1057　〒390　☎0263-57-2569	47, 57
KŌSUKE GOTŌ 後藤 剛助	2-4106 Tsukefune-chō, Niigata-shi, Niigata Pref.　〒951　☎025-222-5550 新潟市附船町2-4106　〒951　☎025-222-5550	48
MASAMITSU KIDO 木戸 雅光	Garden Arashiyama 112, 21-1 Kitatsukurimichi-chō, Sagatenryūji, Ukyō-ku, Kyoto-shi, Kyoto　〒616　☎075-882-3832 京都市右京区嵯峨天竜寺北造路町21-1 ガーデン嵐山112　〒616　☎075-882-3832	49, 77
NAGANO ZŌEN 永野造園	248-3 Sotonakabara-chō, Matsue-shi, Shimane Pref.　〒690　☎0852-21-5898 松江市外中原町248-3　〒690　☎0852-21-5898	50
BUNGOBAYASHI ZŌEN 文吾林造園	3883-3 Kitagata, Iida-shi, Nagano Pref.　〒395-01　☎0265-25-3928 飯田市北方3883-3　〒395-01　☎0265-25-3928	51
EIICHI KAWAYAUCHI 川谷内 映一	6-5-10 Himonya, Meguro-ku, Tokyo　〒152　☎03-710-1258 目黒区碑文谷6-5-10　〒152　☎03-710-1258	53
HIROSHI NAKAMURA 中村 宏	Ōbatake, Tsurumi-ku, Beppu-shi, Ōita Pref.　〒874　☎0977-22-6364 別府市鶴見区大畑　〒874　☎0977-22-6364	55
KEIJI KAJIWARA 梶原 敬司	5-kumi, Minami-suga, Beppu-shi, Ōita Pref.　〒872　☎0977-23-2822 別府市南須賀5組　〒872　☎0977-23-2822	56, 90
UEKŌ 植 孝	260-7 Namiyanagi, Matsumoto-shi, Nagano Pref.　〒390　☎0263-25-2963 松本市並柳260-7　〒390　☎0263-25-3963	59
KŌJI IKEDA 池田 幸司	537-5 Yokoyama-chō, Utsunomiya-shi, Tochigi Pref.　〒320　☎0286-24-4094 宇都宮市横山町537-5　〒320　☎0286-24-4094	60
HIKARI ZŌEN ひかり造園	3-8-9 Takajō, Shizuoka-shi, Shizuoka Pref.　〒420　☎0542-53-6508 静岡市鷹匠3-8-9　〒420　☎0542-53-6508	61
TERUTOSHI IKESHITA 池下 照年	378-6 Higashimura-chō, Fukuyama-shi, Hiroshima Pref.　〒729-02　☎0849-36-1620 福山市東村町378-6　〒729-02　☎0849-36-1620	63
SONOYAMA SHŌUNEN 園山松雲園	212 Uchinakabara-chō, Matsue-shi, Shimane Pref.　〒690　☎0852-24-4618 松江市内中原町212　〒690　☎0852-24-4618	64
SEITAIEN NIWASEI 青苔園 庭清	772-1 Matsuo-shirota, Iida-shi, Nagano Pref.　〒395　☎0265-24-0961 飯田市松尾代田772-1　〒395　☎0265-24-0961	65
NOBUAKI NAGAI 永井 信明	1-22 Kaname-chō, Toshima-ku, Tokyo　〒171　☎03-957-4485 豊島区要町1-22　〒171　☎03-957-4485	66
HIROSHI TERASHITA 寺下 弘	156 Nōka-machi, Ogoto, Ootsu-shi, Shiga Pref.　〒520-01　☎0775-79-1128 大津市雄琴苗鹿町156　〒520-01　☎0775-79-1128	67
SHŪICHI KURIKI 栗木 修一	1-9-24 Nishiki-machi, Ōita-shi, Ōita Pref.　〒870　☎0975-32-7650 大分市錦町1-9-24　〒870　☎0975-32-7650	68
KEIJI MATSUMOTO 松本 啓二	175 Moroenakachō, Kanazawa-shi, Ishikawa Pref.　〒920　☎0762-23-4300 金沢市諸江中丁175　〒920　☎0762-23-4300	69
YŌTARŌ ONO 小野 陽太郎	10 Ōmiya-syakadani, Kita-ku, Kyoto-shi, Kyoto　〒603　☎075-491-4097 京都市北区大宮釈迦谷10　〒603　☎075-491-4097	70, 83
TAKEYUKI ITAKURA 板倉 武幸	2-1-1 Kami-ishihara, Chōfu-shi, Tokyo　〒182　☎0424-85-7195 調布市上石原2-1-1　〒182　☎0424-85-7195	71
TATSUO ISHIKAWA 石川 辰夫	1-8-6 Koinaka, Nishi-ku, Hiroshima-shi, Hiroshima Pref.　〒733　☎082-271-4467 広島市西区己斐中1-8-6　〒733　☎082-271-4467	72
YASUO OKUYAMA 奥山 靖男	866 Ōaza Kirihata, Yamagata-shi, Yamagata Pref.　〒999-22　☎0236-87-4449 山形市大字切畑866　〒999-22　☎0236-87-4449	75
KATSUYA ARAYA 新谷 勝哉	25-14 Koinishi-machi, Nishi-ku, Hiroshima-shi, Hiroshima Pref.　〒733　☎082-271-1663 広島市西区己斐西町25-14　〒733　☎082-271-1663	76
IKECHŪ ZŌEN 池忠造園	3-16 Takara-machi, Kashiwazaki-shi, Niigata Pref.　〒945　☎0257-22-6532 柏崎市宝町3-16　〒945　☎0257-22-6532	78
MASAKI KIKUCHI 菊地 正樹	16-1 Aza Shimo-kōji, Miyatoko, Taiwa-chō, Kurokawa-gun, Miyagi Pref.　〒981-33　☎022-346-2043 宮城県黒川郡大和町宮床字下小路16-1　〒981-33　☎022-346-2043	79
ENDŌ TEIEN SŌSAKUJO 遠藤庭園創作所	1592 Ijimino, Shibata-shi, Niigata Pref.　〒957　☎0254-22-7782 新発田市五十公野1592　〒957　☎0254-22-7782	82
SHŌZŌ ISHIKAWA 石川 昇造	9-42 Mizushima-chō, Niigata-shi, Niigata Pref.　〒950　☎025-244-0998 新潟市水島町9-42　〒950　☎025-244-0998	84
KENKICHI MIFUNE 三船 健吉	12-18 Myōō, Zama-shi, Kanagawa Pref.　〒228　☎0462-53-5189 座間市明王12-18　〒228　☎0462-53-5189	85
TAKAGI ZŌEN 髙木造園	675 Gosanjyō-machi, Hikone-shi, Shiga Pref.　〒522　☎07492-3-7157 彦根市後三条町675　〒522　☎07492-3-7157	91
SHŪZŌ UENO 上野 周三	23 Ōmiya-chō, Saiwai-ku, Kawasaki-shi, Kanagawa Pref.　〒210　☎044-541-2757 川崎市幸区大宮町23　〒210　☎044-541-2757	92, 94
TERUNOBU KINOSHITA 木下 照信	2-12-25 Takaidonishi, Suginami-ku, Tokyo　〒168　☎03-332-7749 杉並区高井戸西2-12-25　〒168　☎03-332-7749	COVER

MAP (DISTRIBUTION)

No.	PREFECTURE(都道府県)	PHOTO NUMBER(写真番号)
❶	IWATE(岩手)	3
❷	MIYAGI(宮城)	31, 79
❸	YAMAGATA(山形)	75
❹	TOCHIGI(栃木)	60
❺	SAITAMA(埼玉)	36, 42, 45, COVER
❻	CHIBA(千葉)	16, 17, 93
❼	TOKYO(東京)	2, 4, 8, 10, 11, 12, 19, 22, 23, 29, 30, 38, 39, 41, 46, 66, 71, 80, 81, 88, 89, 92, 94
❽	KANAGAWA(神奈川)	85
❾	NIIGATA(新潟)	48, 78, 82, 84
❿	ISHIKAWA(石川)	44, 69, 74, 86
⓫	NAGANO(長野)	7, 13, 18, 24, 28, 33, 34, 37, 43, 47, 51, 52, 54, 57, 58, 59, 65
⓬	SHIZUOKA(静岡)	14, 15, 53, 61, 87
⓭	SHIGA(滋賀)	26, 67, 91
⓮	KYOTO(京都)	1, 20, 21, 35, 40, 70, 77, 83
⓯	HYŌGO(兵庫)	49, 73
⓰	SHIMANE(島根)	5, 50, 62, 64
⓱	HIROSHIMA(広島)	6, 63, 72, 76
⓲	ŌITA(大分)	25, 27, 32, 55, 56, 68, 90
⓳	OKINAWA(沖縄)	9

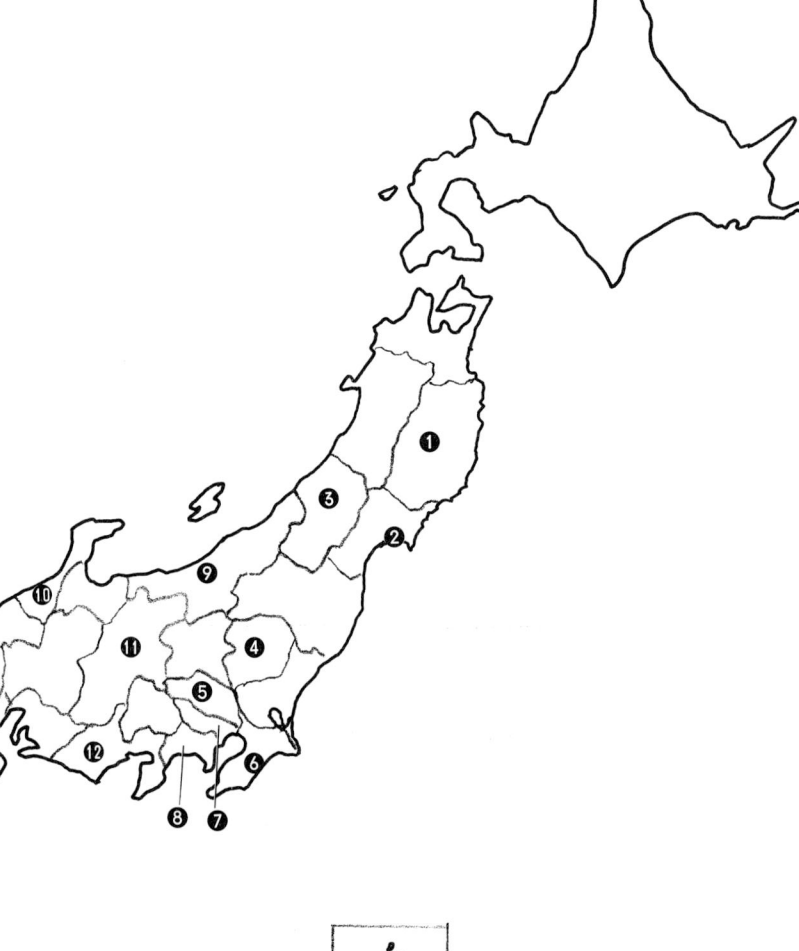

AFTERWORD

What types of gardens are being built now in Japan anyway? And by whom and where? This is a book trying to answer such questions.

In the first place, the Japanese garden has its own characteristic beauty. It has a unique technique, rarely seen elsewhere, of creating a new world while appreciating the charm of nature we all experience in life. It is not a mere production of a miniature of nature. Instead, it is an attempt to bring her charm close to us by way of reorganizing the essential elements of the scene of nature.

It is not, therefore, the question of the available space primarily. The Japanese type of garden may be produced under any environmental circumstances. The Japanese gardening techniques that have been fostered during the long history are now calling the attention not only in Japan but throughout the world.

あ と が き

現代の日本でつくられている庭とは、一体、どんなものか？ 一体、どんな場所でどんな人たちによってつくられているか？ それを紹介する本がこれです。

日本の庭は独特の美しさを持っています。自然の姿を尊びながら、新しい自然の世界を生み出すテクニックは世界にもあまり例を見ません。それは決して風景のミニチュアをつくるというだけではありません。風景の要素を再構成して、身近に潤いを得ようとしているのです。

従って、スペースの広い狭いが問題ではなく、どんな環境の中にあっても、日本式の庭は生み出すことができるのです。長い歴史の中で培われてきた日本の作庭技術は、いま日本だけでなく世界的に注目されています。この本が参考になれば幸いです。

庭 GARDEN VIEWS I
— MODERN JAPANESE GARDENS —

First Edition November 1989

Planner & Editor : Takenosuke Tatsui (Tatsui Teien Kenkyujo)
Kobayashi Kensetsu Bldg. 2-1-28 Nishi-waseda,
Shinjuku-ku, Tokyo 169
Tel.03-202-5233 Fax.03-202-5394
Publisher : Eihachirō Baba
Published : Kenchiku Shiryō Kenkyusha, Ltd.
Tokyū Nishi No.3 Bldg. 1-15-7 Nishi-ikebukuro,
Toshima-ku, Tokyo 171
Tel.03-986-3239   Fax.03-987-3256
Printed : Toppan Printing Co., Ltd.

All rights reserved. No part of this book may be produced or used in any form or by any means without written permission from the publisher. A reviewer may quote brief passages.

ISBN4-87460-206-1

庭 GARDEN VIEWS I
—現代日本の庭—

1989年11月30日　初版発行

企画・編著者：龍居竹之介（龍居庭園研究所）
東京都新宿区西早稲田 2-1-28 小林建設ビル 2 F　〒169
Tel.03-202-5233 Fax.03-202-5394
発　行　者：馬場瑛八郎
発　行　所：株式会社 建築資料研究社
東京都豊島区西池袋 1-15-7 藤久西 3 号館 8 F　〒171
Tel.03-986-3239 Fax.03-987-3256
印　刷　所：凸版印刷株式会社

〈禁無断複製〉　　ISBN4-87460-206-1